junior knowledge
photography

Contents

- 3 All kinds of photographers
- 5 The secret of the black box
- 6 Cameras, films and sizes
- 12 Exposure meters — what are they for?
- 16 Depth of field
- 17 Adequate lighting — photography with flash
- 20 A studio at home: artificial light photography
- 21 How to avoid trouble . . .
- 21 Long live automation
- 22 Photography — black-and-white and colour
- 25 The film has been exposed — now what?
- 26 Using filters
- 27 Handling the camera
- 29 Photographs need to be kept in order
- 30 Sports photography
- 31 Remedies against camera shake
- 32 Lenses for special jobs
- 33 Composing with the camera
- 34 Height, breadth and depth
- 38 Subjects — and what you must remember in choosing them

Hans R. Schatter

Translated by Margaret Baker

Photographs:
Agfa-Archiv (10, 11); R. Döring (11); H. Kanne (36, 37); S. Klement (28); Krölmerz (36); R. Langenberger (8); S. Merkel (40); K. Ott (4, 5, 12, 13, 22, 23, 25, 27, 35); W. Sack (3, 27, 30); H. R. Schatter (10, 15, 16, 17, 18, 20, 21, 24, 32, 33, 34, 36, 41); Schlundt (29); E. Trumler (35).

ISBN 0 7188 2048 7

© 1971 BLV Verlagsgesellschaft mbH, München

© 1973 English Translation, Lutterworth Press

Filmset by BAS Printers Limited, Wallop, Hampshire, England
Printed in Germany

Lutterworth Press . Guildford and London

All kinds of photographers

There are various ways of becoming a camera owner. Perhaps someone in the family decides that it is high time some decent holiday pictures were taken and pops off to the nearest camera shop to buy an Instamatic. Or perhaps you are due for a present and are asked what camera you would like. Here, of course, there are problems. You can't ask for the most expensive for that could cost several hundred pounds. What about the cheapest? It will certainly take pictures for you but its controls are so simple that, although you will find photography fun at first, you will soon discover that there is little chance of developing further as a photographer. Or perhaps the choice is between an automatic camera and one which has to be set and focused for each picture. By the time you have finished reading this book, you will know what to answer.

The many figures which appear on a non-automatic camera are scales which are all closely related. If symbols or letters were used instead of figures, everything would seem less complicated. In practice however things are not complicated at all. You simply set the camera by placing certain figures together and then take the photograph. The photograph can be altered by using different combinations of figures. The first step towards enjoying photography is choosing the right camera for the kind of photography you want to do — otherwise you will be disappointed and your new camera will be a waste of money.

You can learn a lot about photography if you have parents, relations or friends who are amateur photographers. Such enthusiasts are easily recognizable. They are not the sort of people who fish their cameras out of the back of the cupboard for their summer holidays only or merely to take a few family snaps each year. These occasional photographers are referred to, rather scornfully, by amateur photographers as snapshooters. We aren't interested in them. Someone who is happy to take purely souvenir pictures doesn't need to know anything about his camera, exposure times or f numbers. Family photographs are intended to remind us of people and places and it doesn't matter a bit if Aunt Mary has too much light on her cheek or Peter's ears are sticking out. Even the stiff poses and forced expressions do not detract from a picture's value as a family record. But no one will deny that a photograph

The author

Cover picture:
Self-portraits in a mirror are not at all easy. We have to double the distance from the camera to the mirror. With a rangefinder you focus on the mirror image. Lighting is best from the side. Mirror pictures taken in car hub caps, glass balls on the Christmas tree and in driving mirrors are fun to do, as they produce comic distortions.

The majority of photographs taken are holiday pictures. The whole family in front of the Leaning Tower of Pisa, Christine on the beach at Brighton and so on. Someone who goes on a voyage of discovery with a "photographer's eye" can however bring back pictures "with a difference".

which shows a real situation in a family's life, an actual happening observed by the camera, is much more realistic and exciting.
Perhaps somebody makes a movement which is quite unconscious but very characteristic of that particular person — a movement he would have suppressed, had he known he was being photographed. But an unexpected photograph, a snapshot, can preserve this situation for ever. Expert photographers are not dependent to any large extent on expensive cameras and extensive equipment but rather on the quality of the person behind the camera. The finished photograph reveals not only the subject photographed but also something about the person who took the picture. Was it a snapshooter, a good amateur or an artist? There are ten-year-old amateurs, sixty-year-old snapshooters and — at any age level — a very few artists. The following pages are devoted to photography and offer many useful tips to help you use your camera well, they also show that for skilled photography you don't need to be first in maths. Interest, enthusiasm and imagination are important and, if you read this book, you will find that it is all really very simple and clear.

The cost of a bad photograph in terms of film, developing and printing is the same as that of a good one, but the pleasure and admiration earned by a successful shot are infinitely greater.

The secret of the black box

There would be no photographs without light and without a camera which can record our subject on a layer of film sensitive to light.
Let's have a look at the camera first. Whether it is simple or complex, expensive or cheap, it is always a light-tight box with an opening through which light can be allowed to pass for a specified time, and with a device which holds the film flat against the back wall. Every camera has a lens which ensures that it is not merely light but an actual image of the subject which reaches the film. The opening or aperture through which the light passes can be made smaller or larger by means of a diaphragm, and we control the length of time during which the light reaches the film by means of the shutter. We determine what actually appears on the film, the view we select, by means of the viewfinder. When one picture has

Black and white or colour? Compare these two pictures and make up your own mind.

Automatic cartridge camera

Automatic miniature camera with viewfinder

Twin lens reflex camera

miniature single-lens reflex camera

Cameras, films and sizes

Sub-miniature cameras are not only for spies. These minute cameras with a picture size of 8 × 11 mm (Minox) and 12 × 17 mm are used as photographic notebooks. For skilled amateur photographers they do not offer sufficient range.

Cartridge cameras have a film size of 28 × 28 mm. With these cameras, winding the film back after exposure is eliminated and so is everything else which makes inserting the film difficult. Available with automatic exposure and flash cubes that do not need batteries.

There are two types of camera in the 24 × 36 mm size:

Non-reflex miniature cameras with a viewfinder and fixed lens, often with a coupled exposure meter. They are simple to use, light and handy. More expensive models often possess fully automatic exposure control.

Single-lens reflex cameras, picture size 56 mm × 56 mm, as available with through-the-lens metering, interchangeable lenses, very short shutter speeds. They can be used in nearly every area of photography, including macro- and micro-photography.

Twin-lens reflex cameras, picture size 56 mm × 56 mm, in effect two cameras in one: a viewing camera with an ever open diaphragm and the camera proper in which the film is exposed.

Single-lens reflex cameras, picture size 56 mm × 56 mm, as perfected as the miniature reflex cameras, professional models which are correspondingly dear to buy and to use.

Cartridge films are simple to insert. When the last shot has been taken, the film is wound back a little. Then the cartridge can be removed and handed over for processing.

Miniature films (36 and 20 exposures) have a perforated edge which is engaged by the film transport. Supplied in light-tight cassettes. The film must be wound back after exposure.

Roll films (12 exposures 56 × 56 mm) used in 6 × 6 or 6 × 9 cameras. They are wound from their spool on to an empty spare spool. So that the film is not fogged by light outside the camera, it is backed with light-proof paper.

been taken, then the film transport draws an unexposed section of film into position for the next shot. A special catch prevents double exposures.

It is the lens which insures that our picture is in focus. However, unsharp pictures may be caused by several things: the subject may have been moving too quickly; we may not have been holding the camera steady; or perhaps the lens was not properly focused for a particular situation.

The lens' job is to collect and to concentrate light rays so that an image of the subject appears in miniature on the film. The rays of light are brought together at a point which lies behind the focal plane. This point is called the focal point of the lens. The distance between the axis of the lens and the focal point is called the focal length (illustration page 8). The focal length of each lens is engraved on its mount, which also tells us what the light-passing power of the lens is or, in photographic jargon, how fast it is. This is calculated by dividing the focal length by the diameter of the aperture at its widest opening. The result is known as the f number. The lens aperture can be made smaller by the diaphragm. The smaller the aperture, the smaller the amount of light that can reach the film. We therefore have to give a longer exposure. It is similar to a water supply. If we want to fill a jar with water, we can either turn the tap on full and fill the jar quickly; or we can turn it on only slightly and fill the jar slowly. With the diaphragm we can control exactly how much light is admitted. The diaphragm scale can cause confusion because people do not understand what it means. We see "2–2.8–4–5.6–8–11–16–22–32–45". The important thing to remember is that the lower the figure, the larger the aperture it represents; that an f number of 2 is bigger than one of 16. The f numbers are arranged so that each time you move from one f number to the next higher one, the amount of light passed by the lens is halved.

Back to the example of the water. If we compare the diaphragm to a tap which can allow a lot of water to pass or just a little, then we can control turning the "water" on and off with the camera's shutter and fix exactly the length of time during which the film is exposed to the light. We can either expose the film for a short time to a lot of light or for a long time to very little light.

We cannot choose either of these alternatives without careful thought. It depends on whether the subject of our photograph is moving and would be blurred with a long exposure; on whether the camera can be held sufficiently steady to prevent the picture

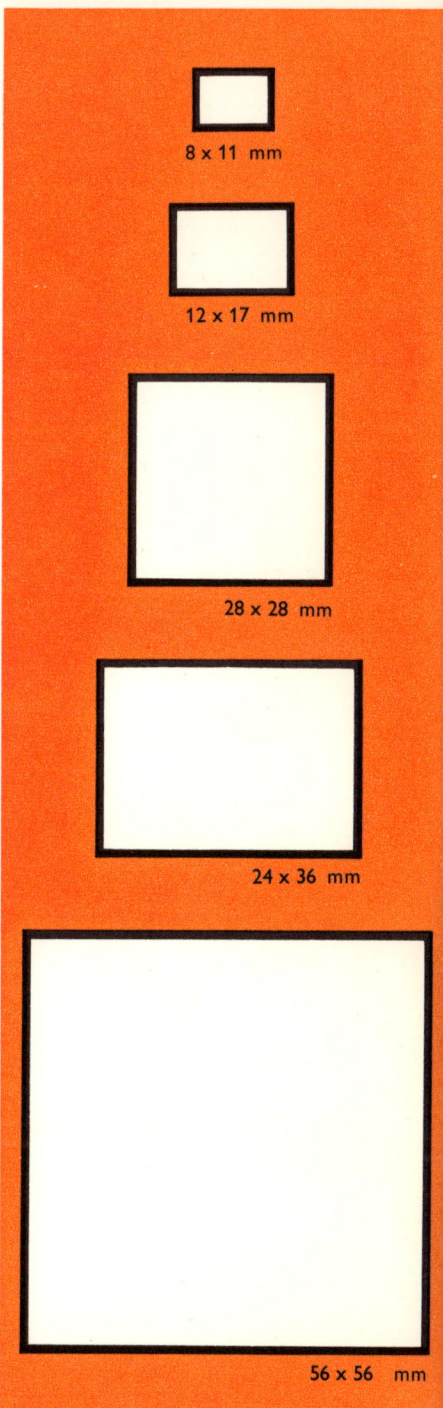

8 x 11 mm

12 x 17 mm

28 x 28 mm

24 x 36 mm

56 x 56 mm

Speeds for stopping movement	
moving clouds	1/15 –1/30
children playing	1/30 –1/60
distant street scenes	1/30 –1/60
people moving	1/60 –1/125
bicyclists, slow	1/60 –1/125
buses and cars	1/60 –1/125
sports photos	1/250–1/500
railway	1/250–1/500
skaters	1/125–1/250
skiers	1/250–1/500

Movement towards or away from the camera – slower speed
Movement obliquely towards the camera – faster speed
Movement across the field of vision of camera – even faster speed

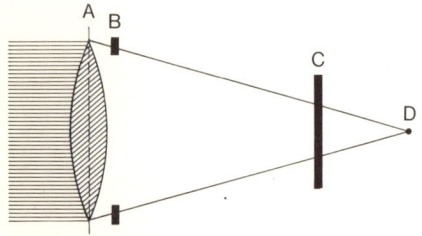

A = lens axis
B = diaphragm
C = focal plane (film)
D = focal point
The distance A–D = focal length

from being spoiled by camera shake; and on the problem of depth of field which we will go into later. For lack of sharpness can be caused by subject movement, camera shake and poor focusing.

The shutter scale is arranged so that the next higher number means a halving of the exposure time. Each number is in fact the bottom half of a fraction and 60 is really 1/60th second. The shutter speeds run like this:

1000–500–250–125–60–30–15–8–4–2–1–B

With the B(rief time) setting the shutter remains open as long as the release is pressed.

Exposure times as long as 1/60th second – 1/125th if you want to be quite safe – can easily be hand-held without camera shake. Very steady photographers can even manage 1/30th, but even they need tripods and cable releases for needle-sharp pictures at longer exposures.

Many cameras also have a delayed-action release or self-timer with a delay of about 10 seconds, so that the photographer can include himself in the picture. The self-timer also makes it possible to take shake-free pictures from a tripod without using a cable release.

Whether we are using a cable release or making a hand-held shot, the actual pressing of the release is important. Press the release gently – practise this without a film in the camera – until you feel a slight resistance. By taking up the slack of the release mechanism in this way our finger has only a short distance to travel to release the shutter and the risk of camera shake is thus considerably lessened. The actual way you hold the camera, too, is decisive in obtaining sharp pictures. The arms should be braced against the body, and you should stand either with the legs apart or with one leg in advance of the other. Standing on one leg or like a tightrope-walker may look more elegant but will result in blurred pictures. We must be careful too to hold the camera straight.

It is fairly easy to estimate time but it is much more difficult to judge the strength of light. Of course, practical experience will help to eliminate completely wrong exposures, but the safest solution is an exposure meter. Unlike our eyes the meter does not adapt itself to changing light conditions.

The exposure meter gives us a range of shutter speed-*f* number combinations which all result in the same effective exposure. And the exposure meter is programmed to give a well-exposed picture

A landscape photograph which is full of feeling — an abiding joy to anyone who knows the locality. It could become a more personal souvenir if friends or acquaintances were included.

of medium contrast. If we point it at the lighter part of the subject, then it will suggest different combinations from those it would offer if pointed at the darker parts of the same subject. So if we point the meter at the sky, we shall get exposures which are too short.

Before it can be used, the exposure meter must be set to the speed of the film you are using. This, for example, is what an exposure meter looks like when it is set to a film speed of 50 ASA:

f number	2	2.8	4	5.6	8	11	16
Shutter speed	1000	500	250	125	60	30	15

From this table we can now make our choice. If we are making a hand-held shot, then there is no question of using anything less than $f.8$ at 1/60. Whether this speed will work or not depends on what we are photographing. If we are dealing with a landscape with no movement, then this combination has the advantage of

Equipment you should have:

Essential:
a camera (protected by an ever-ready case)
a film

Desirable:
exposure meter
lens hood

Extras:
filter
tripod and cable release
flash gun

A hundred years ago a photographer's equipment weighed 54 kg. Things are different today — an automatic camera produces properly exposed, unblurred pictures and is not much bigger than a cigarette pack.

giving a good range of sharpness from the foreground right into the distance. If, however, we wanted to take birds in flight with this shutter speed, then we would end up with only a few wispy blurs on the picture. For this we need at least 1/250 second. Even if we are trying to photograph people walking quickly, we will not succeed with 1/60. 1/125, on the other hand, will capture them without any movement blur. It's worthwhile at this point to note the following: the further an object is from us, the slower the shutter speed that can be used, even though it is moving fast. An example: children running at 5 m distance — 1/125, 10 m — 1/60, 25 m — 1/30. Town traffic at 5 m — 1/125, 10 m and beyond — 1/60. On the other hand, there are situations where we need movement blur. A raging waterfall should not be frozen on our picture, nor should surging waves "congeal".

If it is possible, let us begin by selecting the shutter speed. Short exposure times (1/125 or 1/500) prevent movement blur and camera shake.

So, we now have a short exposure time, we haven't jarred the camera in pressing the release and our subject hasn't moved — but in spite of all this our picture isn't sharp, or rather, not everything in our picture is sharp. And unfortunately the very thing which was most important in the picture is out of focus. In order to understand and to prevent this, we must look into the question of depth of field. This is controlled by the lens of our camera and by the f number. Although the picture is always sharp in the camera viewfinder, the picture on the film may be unsharp because of incorrect focusing. For an important factor for depth of field is the distance between the object and the camera. With mirror-reflex cameras the picture which later appears on the film can be viewed through the lens and you can see exactly what will be in, and what out of, focus. With other cameras we need a rangefinder. Two images side by side have to be brought together. Simple cameras have fixed-focus lenses. They are computed so that from about 2 m to infinity everything is sharp. With automatic cameras we set symbols which correspond to particular distances.

Portraits	Groups	Landscapes
about 1.30 m	about 3 m	from 10 m

With a viewfinder camera we can actually see, once we have established the distance by measurement or estimation, how far the depth of field extends. When we set the distance on the focusing ring, the engraved scale shows us how much depth of field there is for each *f* number. Although there is little room for manoeuvre with a wide aperture, the more we stop down the greater the depth of field. Every *f* number is engraved to the right and the left of the focusing mark. The eight on its side is called "infinity".

$$\xleftarrow[16 - 11 - 4\ \ -2.8 - 4\ \ -11 - 16]{1.8 - 2.3 - 3.5 - 4\ \ -5.2 - 15 - \infty}\xrightarrow{}$$

We can see that with *f*4 the depth of field extends from 3.5 m to 5.2 m, while with *f*11 from 2.3 m to 15 m.

It is on the increased depth of field obtained by stopping down that the "zone focusing" of snapshot cameras is based.

f 8	Distance set to	Sharp from
near	4 m	3 m to 6.5 m
far	10 m	5 m tp ∞

These settings allow the subject plenty of room and allow us to take snapshots without any worry — for a relatively large area will be sharp.
It is important, of course, to be able to estimate distances properly. It is useful if we can compare the distance we are estimating with one we already know and can visualize easily, such as the length of a piece of furniture or of a room we see every day.

Wedding pictures used to be a longwinded business in days gone by. Hidden under a black cloth behind a great box, the photographer focused his apparatus, cried "Watch the birdie!" and captured the solemn faces of the young couple on his glass plate. Often, after some anxious moments of preparation, he burned a quantity of flash powder during the exposure. In his time oval pictures were the latest thing.

There is much pleasure in recording in a photograph the world around us without being noticed. This produces living, dynamic pictures which are much more realistic than formally posed photographs. The snapshot-setting or zone-focusing enables you to react in a split second.

A modern exposure meter
The needle points to a number on the scale. This number (here it is 7) is matched against the indicator on the left, and on the right there are two scales from which a series of *f* number-shutter speed combinations can be read off (here the series runs 8–125, 11–60, 5.6–250).

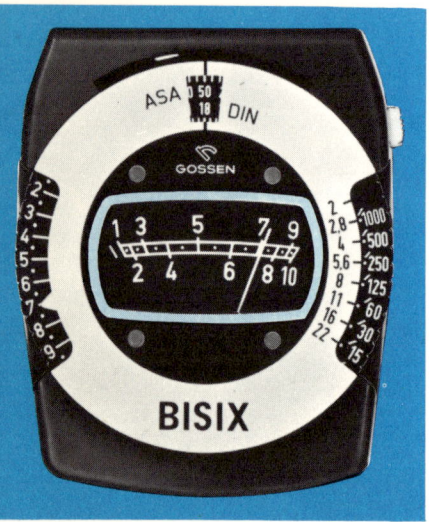

Exposure meters – what are they for?

The photo-electric exposure meter – correctly set to the right film speed and properly handled – is of great help in obtaining accurately exposed pictures. It is objective and so also shows up unintentional errors. While we can estimate distances more or less accurately, our eyes let us down badly when it comes to estimating brightness. They adjust to changing light conditions so that the apparent brightness remains the same, although the actual brightness may be changing dramatically. For example, when we go into a cinema on a sunny day, we can hardly see anything as we enter the auditorium. Our eyes have to adjust to the dimmer light conditions and then we can see both film and cinema without difficulty. When later we come out of the darkness and into the daylight, we are dazzled and our eyes must readjust. The eye adjusts by reducing or enlarging the iris, and we can do the same thing with a camera by opening up or stopping down the diaphragm. With automatic cameras the diaphragm is automatically opened or closed by means of a measured light-value. With non-automatic cameras we carry out this task with the help of our exposure meter. In addition we have the opportunity of making changes in order to give our pictures a brighter or darker character. We can choose between two methods of using an exposure meter: reflected-light metering, when the brightness of the subject is measured from the camera position, and incident-light metering in which the light falling on the subject is measured from the subject position. With most exposure meters a diffusing attachment must be placed over the light-sensitive cell. With reflected-light meters the following should be borne in mind. Do not include too much sky when you point your meter at a landscape but direct the meter slightly downwards or shade it with your hand. With subjects that have areas of extreme light and shade, and so a high degree of contrast, the light and dark areas must be measured separately. In this way a middle value can be obtained — with colour reversal film this is always the way to expose so that the brightest areas still retain detail. Often the shadows must be lightened with the help of a reflector or flash. In order to set the exposure meter without trouble, we need to test its reliability and

Reflected-light method

Incident-light method

1. Rapid film winding lever
2. Exposure counter
3. Shutter speed dial
4. Shutter release button
5. Exposure meter window
6. Depth-of-field scale
7. Focusing ring
8. Diaphragm setting ring
9. Film rewind crank

Single-lens reflex camera with interchangeable lens

calibrate it. The camera shutter, the film material and the exposure meter all have their own tolerances which may add up or cancel each other out. To check this, we make three test exposures of a subject with medium contrast, without altering the f number. Shot No. 1 is taken according to the meter, No. 2 at the next faster speed and No. 3 at the next slower speed. If shot No. 1 gives the best result, then the exposure meter is working properly. If shot No. 2 is better, then the meter is giving speeds which are too long. We can therefore in the future set the meter to 100 ASA for a 50 ASA film. Accordingly, if shot No. 3 is the best, then set the meter to 25 ASA instead of 50 ASA. This correction will be valid for all types of film.

The exposure meters built into cameras must also be directed accurately towards the subject from the camera position. Tilting the camera can falsify the meter reading. In taking photographs against the light on colour reversal film we increase the f number the meter suggests by one stop.

Rules of thumb (for those who don't own an exposure meter):

F 8, 1/60 second with a 50 ASA film, for full sunshine. When the sky is clouded, the exposure is doubled. And so, in order to have an unblurred picture, we open up the diaphragm!

Anyone who has a camera without either automatic exposure or an exposure meter should buy a photo-electric exposure meter as the most important camera accessory. The cost is balanced out by its accuracy, reliability and the many correctly exposed pictures it enables you to take.

The effect of a picture is greatly influenced by the position of the camera. In the first picture we have the usual shot. In the second the photographer has gone down on one knee and the cobbles form the foreground and become part of the picture. The colour picture shows only a section of a building and it is impossible to recognize where the locality is.

Depth of field

Pictures must be sharp. The foreground as well as the background. This is no problem if you follow the guidance of the depth-of-field scale on the camera. If we want something which is 20 m from the camera to be sharp, then we set the focus to 20 m. This does not mean that things which are 19.80 or 20.40 m distant will be out of focus, for every camera renders a certain area sharp. This area is the depth of field. Its depth depends on the aperture chosen. The more we stop down, the greater the area of depth of field.

> Focus on ∞ (infinity)
> Foreground out of focus — background sharp
> Focus on an object in the foreground
> Foreground sharp — background out of focus

Using the depth of field means reading from the depth-of-field scale how far it extends for a particular f number. In this area everything will be sharp. So that it works when you are on the job, practise focusing according to the depth-of-field scale.

The most important part of our picture must also be the sharpest. Another way to calculate our depth of field is according to this formula: multiply the nearer distance by two and divide the focal length of the lens by this number.

For example: Focal length 50 mm. We want to calculate a field of sharpness from 5 m to infinity: $5 \times 2 = 10$. $50 \div 10 = 5$. But as f 5 is not provided on the camera, use f 4 or f 5.6.

If we want a particular area to be sharp, we must remember that one-third of the depth of field lies in front and two-thirds behind the distance set.

The exposure meter gives us a range of shutter speed-aperture combinations. From this we choose the combination which will give us the desired depth of field, on condition, however, that we do not have too long an exposure time which would cause subject movement and run the risk of camera shake. In doubtful cases we must sacrifice some of the depth of field. It is often very effective when the subject stands out sharply against a less sharp background.

Under-exposed pictures give an evening effect. Over-exposed pictures lose whole areas of detail. This can be seen clearly in these pictures by studying the clouds.

Adequate lighting – photography with flash

Flash light is of very short duration. In order to get a picture, the moment of the flash must coincide exactly with the time during which the shutter is open. The shutter and the firing of the flash must be synchronized (*synchron*=at the same time).
In the early days one normally burnt magnesium powder. Then came flash bulbs – or flash cubes which allow four flashes. The bulb is fired by an electric current from a battery inside the flash gun.
The flash gun has to be synchronized with the camera shutter. Many flash guns are so constructed that they can be attached to the centre contact in the camera's accessory shoe. Or the flash gun is linked by a cable to the X-contact.
Once the flash gun is in position, we need to set the shutter speed. For flash bulbs at 1/25 or 1/30 second. For electronic flash guns the time lies between 1/25 and 1/125. The instruction leaflet that comes with the camera will give the necessary information. Whereas a flash bulb can only be used once, an electronic flash provides us with a whole series of flashes. The duration of the flash is very short: 1/500 to 1/2000 second.
Light falls off as a square of its distance. This means that if you double the distance between the subject and the flashgun, the amount of light reaching the subject is reduced to a quarter (not a half as you might think). You must therefore open up the diaphragm to admit four times as much light, so the aperture is increased by two stops.
Every flash gun has a specific guide number which helps us to settle on the correct distance or f number.

$$\text{Guide number} = \text{distance} \times f \text{ number}$$
$$\text{Distance} = \frac{\text{guide number}}{f \text{ number}} \qquad f \text{ number} = \frac{\text{guide number}}{\text{distance}}$$

Let's suppose that the guide number of our flash gun or flash bulb is 30 for 50 ASA film speeds, and that the subject we are taking is 4 metres away. Then we calculate as follows: $30 \div 4 = 7.5$.

It is difficult to avoid converging verticals if you only have a simple camera, but they are less disturbing if you enlarge just a section of an architectural photograph. Even with the picture of the church tower seen through the window, the frame does have sloping verticals but they have been trimmed. Windows and doorways are popular ways of framing pictures.

We therefore need an aperture of *f* 8. We can from this work out what distances the various *f* numbers allow:

30 = *f* 8 × 3.7 m 30 = *f* 5.6 × 5.3 m
30 = *f* 11 × 2.8 m 30 = *f* 4 × 7.5 m

Guide numbers are based on the law that light falls off as a square of the distance. You will find tables of guide numbers for various film speeds on the flash bulb or cube cartons or in the instructions that come with electronic flash guns.

Before we fire off our flash, we must remember that front lighting gives flat pictures without any modelling. For snapshots, where speed is of the first importance, the flash gun is handiest on the camera, but better lighting is obtained through having the flash at the side. For this we need an extension cable between the camera and the flash gun. We can get a very soft lighting by using bounce flash. For this the flash gun is pointed towards the ceiling. The light is then reflected back by the white surface. This indirect lighting does, of course, mean some wastage of light. We therefore open up the diaphragm by two or three stops to get a strength of light similar to direct flash.

A rule of thumb for exposure for bounce flash in the living room divide the guide number by 7; in very small, light-coloured rooms, bathroom and kitchen, divide by 5.

If we want to take portraits by flash and, to achieve good modelling, fire the flash from an arm stretched obliquely to one side, then we can lighten the shadow side with a white reflecting surface such as a projection screen, a white cloth or a large drawing pad.

To make the fullest use of flash, there is no need to wait until it is dark. We can use flash as fill-in lighting in daylight and lighten subjects at a distance of 1.5 to 4 metres which are affected by hard shadows in direct sunlight. By this means the pictures become brighter and more colourful. We work out the camera-subject distance, set the aperture, which is obtained from the guide number, and then meter the exposure and set the appropriate shutter speed. If you want the background to be darker, you shorten the exposure time by one stop – 1/125 instead of 1/60. While the flash has its full effect, the sunlight will be weakened by the shorter exposure time.

Example: Distance 4 m, guide number 24 – *f* 5.6
  Exposure meter reading at *f* 5.6, 1/125 second
  Camera settings: *f* 5.6, 1/125 second, 4 m distance

Above left:
There are several ways of giving a picture a feeling of depth. Parallel lines seem to come together in the distance. If the photographer stands at an angle to such lines, then there is a fine impression of depth. In this picture it is emphasized by the towering pillars.

Below left:
Reflections in water can produce happy effects. In this picture note the diagonal composition. An exposure must be chosen to make the most of the ripples in the water.

Above right:
In colour photography the best colour is obtained when the sun is behind the camera. In against-the-light photographs the dark shadow side of the subject is towards the camera. In our case the sun is shining through young green leaves. The comparatively large foreground area allows the tree shadow to dominate the composition.

Below right:
There is a danger of a blue cast on pictures taken at midday, particularly in Mediterranean countries and by the sea. The photographer has to decide whether he wants a picture with true colouring through the use of a filter or whether he wants to use the blue cast as a creative element in the picture.

Sunshine

f 8–1/125th second at ASA 40–64
= sufficient depth of field
= sufficiently short exposure
= sufficient brightness

Photography with flash is not usually permitted in museums. If you are not specially equipped for museum photography with powerful lenses and high-speed film, then you will have to trust to luck. As you will need long exposures and a wide aperture because of the feeble light, it is a good idea to steady the camera against the wall. The best thing is to try several shutter speeds with the lens fully open. If you get down on the floor, you can obtain a tremendous impression of space.

A studio at home: artificial light photography

For this we can use ordinary household electric light bulbs – this would give fairly long exposure times – or special photographic lamps, which have a shorter life but give very much brighter light. The same rule applies with artificial light as with flash: the light falls off as the square of the distance! In using colour film by artificial light we must bear in mind that artificial light sources have different colour temperatures from daylight. We therefore need special artificial light films when we want to achieve natural-looking colours.

If photographic lamps are to be used, we must check that the electrical mains can bear this loading. If other equipment with a heavy consumption of electricity, such as ovens or electric irons, is run off the same circuit, then the fuses may blow. The load we can place on the mains depends on the rating of the fuses.

If your power sockets are fitted with 13 amp. fuses and your mains' voltage supply is 240, then you can have a loading of up to 3120 watts. A No. 2 photoflood lamp is usually about 500 watts, so the socket will cope with up to six lamps. The most important thing in photography is the correct lighting of the subject. If we light it with a lamp directly from in front, then we will get shadowless illumination. The picture will, of course, be very flat with no modelling. If there is a strong light overhead, the result in a portrait will be deep shadows round the chin, eyes and nose. Lighting from below has a similar effect.

If you are working with two lamps, then the fore and backgrounds can be lit. The main light places the model in the proper light so that his or her form looks attractive and in character. This light also divides the picture into light and shade and so creates dramatic effects.

A second light source – or several other light sources – helps to lighten shadows, produce hair lights, accent facial features and light the background. The secondary lights are put into position only when effective main lighting has been achieved. We can, of course, also make against-the-light photographs with artificial light. For this we need to have camera, subject and lamp in a straight line. The strong contrast of dark and light produces impressive silhouettes. It is important, however, that only the most significant lines are emphasized.

How to avoid trouble...

Cameras do not enjoy being dropped and they are allergic to water. They hate dust, whether inside — dust before you insert the film — or out. We don't want scratches on the film or bits of fluff and sand in the lens mount affects its smooth action.

Our lens does not like being touched — we blow dust off. It is even better if we clean the lens with a lens brush. Then we breathe on the lens and wipe it gently with a cloth or tissue intended for photographic lenses. Never dust it with your handkerchief or the cloth used for cleaning gramophone records!

While not in use, the lens is happiest when protected by a lens cap or by a closed ever-ready case.

Cameras do not like humidity either — sudden temperature changes — for the lens mists over and produces unsharp pictures. It needs to be acclimatized gradually. Wiping the mist away does not help.

Bathing in the full sun or even at the back of a car does not do the camera or its film any good. Both need to be stored somewhere cool and dry.

And should something go really wrong, then under no circumstances should you try to repair it yourself. Lacking the proper tools and technical knowledge, you might only make matters worse.

Long live automation

The photographic industry is always under pressure to ensure that even people who are not interested in photography may take snapshots of good quality. A vibration-free, gentle shutter-release system with minimal camera shake. Instant-loading systems for "people with two left hands".

For those who cannot or will not estimate distances, "Focusing symbols" and for correct exposure, automatic exposure with coloured signals (for example, Agfa cameras).

green	Picture properly exposed
red	Inadequate lighting conditions (use flash or a time exposure)

The upper picture looks like a postcard. But if you stand at the foot of the tower, you have the feeling that the weight of all that steel is pressing down on you, something that the lower picture tries to emphasize.

Photography – black-and-white and colour

The pictures in this book demonstrate that photographs can be taken in colour and also in black and white. While black-and-white photographs – in these the bright colours of nature are transformed into grey tones of varying depth – land up as prints in a photo album, colour photographs can either be colour slides – positive film transparencies – which can be thrown by a slide projector on to a white surface, or colour prints.

Transparencies give a greater depth of colour. But, of course, you cannot alter the size or picture area once the picture has been taken. The most important information on the film packet is, next to the type of film, the speed of the film. This will be given in ASA or, in the case of German films, in DIN. The higher the ASA rating, the faster the film. A 100 ASA film is twice as fast as a 50 ASA film. With a film that is twice as fast, we gain a diaphragm stop. If we

With holiday pictures you don't want to concentrate only on the buildings mentioned in the guide books but should try to catch the characteristic details of the whole area. The crazy roofs of the old houses and the boats on the beach may have more to say about the landscape than the over-photographed village church. Until recently out-of-focus foregrounds were considered a crime, but, as our picture shows, blurred blobs of colour give a feeling of summer.

are using an exposure meter or an automatic camera, then the first thing to do, after loading, is to set the film speed. If we forget to do that, then we will have wrongly exposed films.

By the way, ASA ratings are not indications of quality. The different speeds provide the correct material for different kinds of photograph. The sharper and more detailed a photograph is to be, the slower the film speed. For instance, if we are photographing the inner workings of a clock or a finely veined insect wing in close-up, then we can, as nothing is moving, choose a long exposure time and use a tripod. With a film rated between 8 and 32 ASA we will obtain maximum sharpness.

It is the middle-range films between 40 and 100 ASA that we make most use of. They are universal films for normal lighting conditions and are best suited for all kinds of photography.

If lighting conditions are not adequate, and our lens is not very fast (some miniature cameras have lenses with a speed of f1.4), and the subject is moving too, then we need a very fast film. With them we can photograph in the dim light of theatres, circuses, ice stadia or even by candle light. They are also excellent for taking night shots. Remember, when using faster films, to give adequate

How many ASA make how many DIN?

In the ASA system a doubling of the film speed is shown by a doubling of the ASA number. In the DIN system a rise of three units represents a doubling of the film speed.

25 ASA	15 DIN
40 ASA	17 DIN
50 ASA	18 DIN
100 ASA	21 DIN
125 ASA	22 DIN
400 ASA	27 DIN
640 ASA	29 DIN
1000 ASA	31 DIN

Vertical or horizontal?

Often it is the subject which decides the shape. By emphasizing the vertical format we can direct the eye even more forcefully on to the important feature.

> Every colour picture printed in a book or newspaper is made up of the colours red, blue and yellow. You can see them on the endpapers of this book. In a colour film the light is filtered by layers of complementary colours — blue for yellow, green for red and red for blue.

exposure as they tend to produce very coarse grained negatives. With black-and-white films the shades of colour are converted into grey tones. Which grey corresponds to a particular colour is difficult to determine. A particular red and green can produce almost the same grey tone. The reproduction of colours can be influenced by filters. With black-and-white photography we are chiefly concerned with contrasts in lighting, with the effect of light and shade.

For colour photography there are two types of film: *colour negative film* for colour or black-and-white prints and for transparencies. This produces after development a negative colour picture.

With *reversal film* or *colour slide film* we don't get a negative colour picture, but instead a positive colour transparency. There are daylight reversal films and artificial light reversal films. Colour reversal films must be adequately exposed. In doubtful cases underexposure is not so harmful as overexposure. The colour film consists of three colour-sensitive layers. Each of them is sensitive to one colour — blue, red, green. The development and reversal of the colours are difficult. That is why film manufacturers usually develop transparency films themselves.

When we buy a reversal film, we usually pay for the development at the same time. We simply have to send the exposed film to the processing service of the film factory in the envelope provided. Within a few days the film is returned fully developed. We can order our transparencies to be returned as strips in a protective sleeve or ready for projection in card or plastic mounts. These mounts are glassless.

Colour negative film on the other hand is sold at a price which does not include development. It is available in only one type which can be used for both daylight and artificial light. The adjustment in colour takes place in the laboratory.

Thanks to a special process we can obtain black-and-white prints, colour prints and duplicate transparencies from colour reversal film. There is, however, a considerable loss in quality.

The film has been exposed – now what?

Forests are a treasure house of subject matter. This is where you show whether you are a photographer or not.

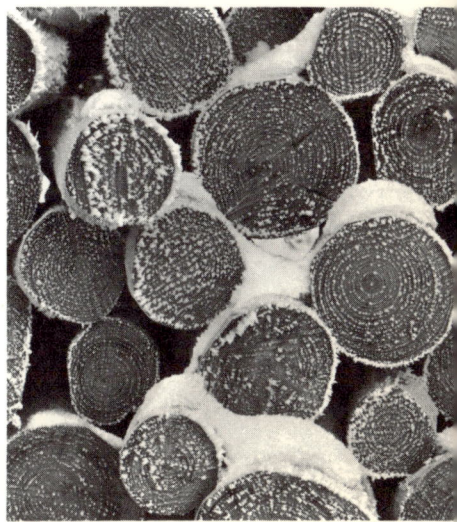

After we have taken it out of the camera, we must wrap it carefully in the silver paper in which the new, unused film was packed, or put it back in its tin canister. An exposed film should never be put unprotected into a pocket. We mustn't leave an exposed film lying round at home but should take it as soon as possible for processing. Colour transparency films are sent by post to a colour laboratory. With black-and-white films we have merely to ask a film processor to develop the film. Then we can see on the negative whether our picture is blurred, whether we have over- or underexposed and which shots are better composed. We don't want to pay out extra money for pictures which have gone wrong. From the negatives we can also decide how to trim the picture to make the greatest impact.

Using filters

Black-and-white films render colours as tones of grey. As a result completely different colours give the same grey tone. Brilliant red flowers are reproduced in almost the same grey as the green of leaves. Here a green filter would make a difference — the flowers would be darker and the leaves lighter.

With filters light is held back. We must therefore lengthen the exposure time or open the diaphragm an equivalent amount. The filter factor which tells you how much extra exposure is required is engraved on the rim of the filter. For colour films only protective filters against ultra-violet rays at high altitudes and polarizing filters against reflections are used.

Yellow filter	increases contrast (winter sports, landscapes, clouds, snow). The black-and-white film would otherwise render the bright blue of the sky as white. Tanned skin becomes lighter. Yellow, green and orange become lighter — blue and violet become darker.
Yellow-green filter	similar but stronger than a yellow filter. Tanned skin is not lightened, green parts of the landscape become lighter. Yellow and green become lighter — violet, blue and red become darker.
Orange to red filter	dramatizes cloud formations. Lessens atmospheric haze at high altitudes. "Contrasty" photographs. Filter factor 3. Skin colour becomes paler. Freckles are cut out.
UV filter	holds back ultra violet rays in mountain and beach photography. Usually used in colour photography as a protection against a blue cast. No increase in exposure.
Polarizing filter	eliminates reflections from non-metallic surfaces. In landscape shots clouds stand out better against the blue sky. Colours are heightened — by the removal of reflections — in colour shots. In general, however, with colour films no filters are used! Filter factor 2–3.

Handling the camera

We are now familiar with the apparatus with which we take our pictures. Before getting involved with picture composition and choice of subject, let's take the camera and the instruction booklet and practise in the proper sequence all the hand movements until they become automatic, for when we are taking photographs we must be able to concentrate wholly on the subject.
We want to get into the habit of carrying out all hand movements in the same order. We can practise putting the film in with a wasted film which the local camera shop can give us.
Inserting a film may go smoothly enough when you are sitting at a

In this picture we can study the rules for using movement blur. When people cross straight in front of us, they are blurred, while those coming obliquely towards us from a corner are still sharp, although moving at the same speed. The lack of sharpness shows that movement is taking place. Compared with this the snapshot opposite seems very static.

Follow this procedure every time:

1. Measure the light
2. Set the aperture
3. Set the shutter speed
4. Focus
5. Take up the slack of the release
6. Make the exposure
7. Wind on

table but cause difficulties when you are standing. We must, therefore, also practise changing a film standing up. When the film is in position, check that the film transport is working properly and set the exposure counter. If the film won't move without being forced, then we have done something wrong and must open the camera again. If the film cannot be turned on after several shots, then we must try to wind the film back (but note which shot we have reached). If that does not work, then we will have to have the film taken out in a camera shop. In most cases, however, inserting the film is child's play and works well. It is important always to do this job in the shadow of a house, a tree or, if necessary, of your own body.

Before you open the camera, always check whether or not there is a film inside and remember to wind the film back before opening the camera.

By the way, the longer the focal length used, the greater the danger of camera shake. As a rule of thumb, remember that the shutter speed should correspond to the focal length, and so with a 50 mm lens use 1/50 second, with a 135 mm lens 1/125 second. For this reason photography often means dragging a tripod around. Therefore very powerful tele-lenses are heavyweights.

A prize-winning sports photograph.

Photographs need to be kept in order

Many people keep their photographs in an old shoe box which then has to be turned out when a particular picture is needed. With luck it is found, uncrumpled, and without dog ears.

Anyone who wants to have his photographic work readily available, will get himself a photo album and stick his pictures in it, either immovably with photographic paste or with photo-corners which allow a photograph to be taken out again. A photo album will be not only a collection of photographic memories but also a record of our development from photographic beginner to fully fledged amateur. The rules which apply to picture composition are equally valid for the arrangement of pictures in an album. And so we do not stick them in higgledy-piggledy but in a thoughtful, orderly fashion. Important or successful photographs should be given plenty of space. Pictures without borders look bigger. Deckle edges are rather old-fashioned now.

We can frame our best pictures and hang them on the wall. Borderless frames, which protect our pictures but do not lessen their impact, are well worth using.

The best place to stand is on a curve, for you mustn't step on to the track, so you need a spot where there is no danger of members of the public straying into the picture at the wrong moment.

Sports photography

Let's imagine a football stadium full of people, and on the field an exciting game between two top teams.
We want to get out our camera and record the game but before doing so let's check where the sun is. However attractive against-the-light photographs may be, this kind of lighting is not suitable for a football match. Of course, it will be decided before the game begins which players must play against the sun in the first half, and

which in the second. For our purpose oblique front lighting is the most favourable. As photo-reporters we must ask ourselves "What do we want to say photographically about this particular match?" If we want to show that so many thousand people are crowded on the terraces, then we must show the field and the terraces. Every black spot is a human head. The many spots give an idea of the size of the stadium and the number of spectators. But we won't find Mr Brown from the house next door in this confusion of spots. If we decide on half the terrace and the edge of the football field, then it is possible to recognize individual details. Anyone who has seen the whole stadium has obtained a sufficiently good idea of whether it is half empty or packed full. With the terrace shot the photographer can cheat a bit however. If he photographs a place on the terraces which affords particularly good viewing conditions and which even when the crowd is small is fully occupied, then he may write underneath: "The packed stadium...", and only professionals will know that that particular spot is always full.
In close-up shots the surroundings disappear altogether. We distinguish only the absorbed face of a football fan. There is nothing to be seen of the field.
And even if the caption tells us that this is a football match the spectator could just as well be at an athletics meeting.

Film expiry date

A date is printed on the film carton. Up to this date the film manufacturer guarantees the film. Date-expired film is often sold as a special offer. If it has been stored in good, cool, dry conditions, any film can be used several months after the date stated. With colour films, however, you can only overstep the limit by a few months. Colour film which has been stored for too long produces pictures with thin colour.

Remedies against camera shake

The best guarantee against blurred pictures is offered by tripods and cable releases. What, snapshots with a tripod? We must find other ways. To make sure that our own bodies are not the cause of camera shake, we must deaden the pressure on the release through counter-pressure.
One possibility, for photographs inside buildings where one ought not to use tripods, is to adjust the camera, press it up against a wall or door, and then take up the slack of the release and make the exposure.
For low-level shots, kneel down on one knee, with the elbows supported on the other. In the open air fences and walls provide support for the camera during longer exposures.

Lenses for special jobs

The normal focal length corresponds roughly to the diagonal of the negative produced. With the miniature format of 24 × 36 mm it is somewhat longer, namely 50 mm. 85 mm to 135 mm lenses can be called long focus. A 135 mm is a tele-lens.

Lenses with shorter focal lengths, for instance 21 mm or 35 mm, are called wide-angle lenses, for the angle of view which these lenses have is wider than that of a normal lens. The tele-len, on the other hand, has a longer focal length, 90, 135, 200, 300 or more. The angle of view is much narrower. The tele-lens brings distant subjects forward like a telescope.

Tele-lenses from 180 mm to 250 mm and up to 400 mm foreshorten and seem to distort the perspective. They also require a tripod.

Above: wide-angle lenses include more
Middle: normal lens
Below: telephoto lenses bring things nearer

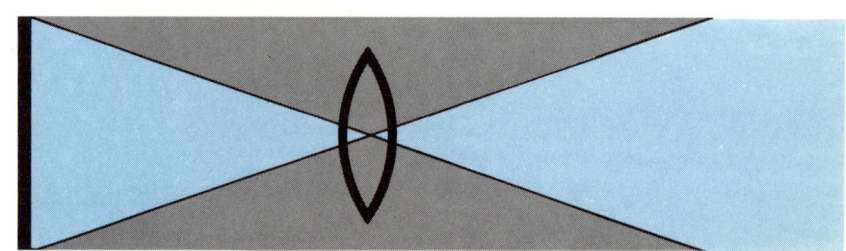

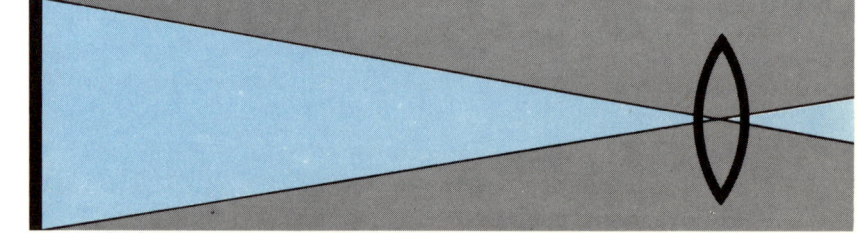

Composing with the camera

Some people are quite happy if the thing they have photographed is recognized later. We are not so easily satisfied. A successful photograph costs just the same as a bad one. And if we keep just a couple of rules in our heads, then we will have photographs we can really take pleasure in.
We determine in the viewfinder what should appear on the picture. But then we don't just press the release. We want to capture the significant character of our subject. Even when taking the most modest of photographs we must make sure that the camera is straight, that our subject dominates the picture, that nothing disturbing intrudes, that no boughs or twigs are growing out of a person's head or nose, or lines passing through his head. If we are not forced to make a snapshot because we want to record a brief dynamic situation, then we can take plenty of time. If possible, we

The background emphasizes how colourful the flowers are. There are two rules to follow in plant photography: go in as close as possible — a single bloom is far more effective than a whole bunch — and choose a simple background. The background should be in subdued colours and out of focus so that it does not distract attention from the main feature. We can check this with the depth-of-field scale on the camera. The same flowers against a bright sky seem less colourful than against a dark background.

Before we press the release button, we must study the habits of the animals we are photographing and should avoid alarming them with sudden movements.

walk around our subject, seeking out the best viewpoints, changing the camera position, kneeling down or finding something to stand on.

A tip: first go in close and then as far back as necessary. We study the light. With black-and-white photography we work with light and shade effects and we can compose very effectively with side or back lighting. For colour pictures front lighting gives the strongest colour effects. That does not mean to say that we can only take colour photographs with front lighting. Side lighting in particular gives satisfactory colour with light-dark effects, and good depth and modelling. We do not want our picture to look too artificial, so we should not concentrate everything into the middle of the picture.

Every subject can be interpreted in different ways. Some, however, are unconvincing, uninteresting, even boring, while others are gripping, unusual, inspiring, fascinating.

One interpretation of a subject is full of feeling and artistry, while another is gripping, uninhibited and disturbing. Let's look at photographs with this in mind, trying to find out what style the photographer concerned or a particular magazine favours.

The personal style of the photographer influences his interpretation of a subject. Our camera is objective only in so far as it records the subject with technical perfection. In the photographer's hands it is a tool with which he makes a visual statement. Just like the brush and paints which a painter needs to compose a painting.

Height, breadth and depth

A photographic image has two dimensions in a print or transparency: height and breadth. But the original subject has three. To height and breadth must be added depth, the distance from the foreground to the background. What means do we have of creating from two dimensions the impression of three dimensions? In considering diaphragm settings and depth of field we have already learnt one possibility: the contrast between what is sharp and what is unsharp. Through a sharp foreground and unsharp background, or unsharp foreground, sharp centre and sharp background, we can contrive an impression of depth and space.

Another indication of depth is given by the overlapping of objects. When – as in the picture on page 36 – the car hides the girl's legs, then the girl is obviously behind the car and so is at a greater distance.

The position of the horizon is particularly important in landscape photographs. The higher the horizon, the greater the appearance of depth in the picture.

The foreground of a picture – usually in the region of the lower edge – is nearer to us. A good way of showing that an object photographed is at a distance is to show it through a frame in the foreground (see page 17).

The foreground always looks darker and distant objects paler. The picture taken through a frame illustrates this also.

There are different shapes for our pictures: the square (this shape is found in 28 × 28 mm 126 cartridge films) and the rectangle. The miniature film (24 × 36 mm) offers us, when the camera is held horizontally, a landscape shape, and an upright shape when it is held vertically. This enables us to compose our pictures in a variety of ways. We can choose a wide, spread-out, peaceful horizontal shape, or a soaring stark upright format. The subject on page 24

In photogenic situations like these there is not much time for thinking, so use the snapshot settings and plenty of film.

Pose people behind the car to make the car look bigger. As the person serves as an indication of scale, a car will look very small if people stand in front of it.

Flash is not usually allowed at circuses, so we must make do with the flood and spot lighting. We need a very fast film (colour films should be artificial-light ones) — and plenty of luck.

You can get particularly lifelike pictures when the people you are taking do not suspect what you are about. Take a whole series of shots if you can.

has its narrowness emphasized by the extremely slim aperture.

A broad landscape picture has its peace and calm accentuated by horizontal lines. Many general views, panoramic photographs, group pictures and wide landscapes are taken in the horizontal format.

Just as horizontal lines increase the effect in a landscape picture, so do vertical lines in the upright format. Narrow ravines, high towers, columns, church towers and lofty rooms are much more effective taken in the upright format.

A properly chosen format allows us to make the best use of the picture's planes and to concentrate the viewer's eyes on the most important objects.

In most photographs there is much too much to see. It is obvious that the photographer was himself not clear as to what he wanted to emphasize. In pictures like these you can certainly see a great deal — but nothing in detail. For this reason we will go in as close as possible to the subject we are photographing and concentrate on significant aspects.

For instance, you can photograph a toy train in a box of sand in such a way that it looks like a real locomotive. If, however, we photograph the engine on an outstretched hand, then no one will believe — however accurate the model — that it will be speeding between London and Newcastle in a few minutes' time. Our photographs must have indications of scale. Best suited for this purpose are things which are very familiar, things whose size we already know well. The best indicator of scale is a person. So that we can find our way around our photograph easily, it should have a certain order. The elements which are important to the picture should stand out well from the less important things. We can achieve this, for example, with a quiet background or an empty sky.

To the visual ingredients of composition such as the contrast between large and small, light and dark, sharp and unsharp, horizontal and vertical, must be added the inner content. After all, our pictures must not merely show something, they must say something too. A picture says something because the people who look at a photograph relate their own beliefs and experiences to it. Only a very few people can look at something in a neutral fashion without allowing their own feelings to be involved.

Light

Front light
flat lighting with hardly any shadow

Side light
more or less heavy cast shadows. Good modelling.

Back light
objects facing the camera are in dark tones

Lens hood

The lens hood is also sometimes called a sun shade, as it first of all prevents the sun from falling directly on to the lens in against-the-light photography. In other kinds of photography the lens hood shields against stray light and reflections coming from the side as well as giving better contrast and protecting the lens from damage. Professional photographers use lens hoods all the time, even when the sky is cloudy. The lens hood also protects against water droplets in rain and snow.

Subjects – and what you must remember in choosing them

Let's photograph that which interests us! This book is intended to give ideas and to offer advice. It doesn't matter if someone else has different views and wants to photograph in a different way. One's personal development as a photographer is more important than rigidly following formal rules.

Photography at the zoo

Watch these points and then the entrance ticket will pay for itself:
1. Don't go too near the bars. Don't climb over barriers and do obey the instructions of the keepers.
2. Seek out the best place to stand so that the usual zoo trappings of bars, ditches and spectators disappear.
3. Don't use a shutter speed any slower than 1/125. Lie in wait and be ready to press the release the instant the right picture comes up. Snapshot-settings will help you to work fast. Use your meter to decide the proper exposure beforehand.
4. Don't be mean with film. Take a whole series of shots.
5. Observe the animals, the way they move and their behaviour.
6. Don't frighten or annoy the animals by noisy shouting or wild movement. Learn to wait.
7. Don't try to photograph zoo animals at weekends and bank holidays. There are days and times when fewer people are about.
8. In some zoos you need special permission to photograph.

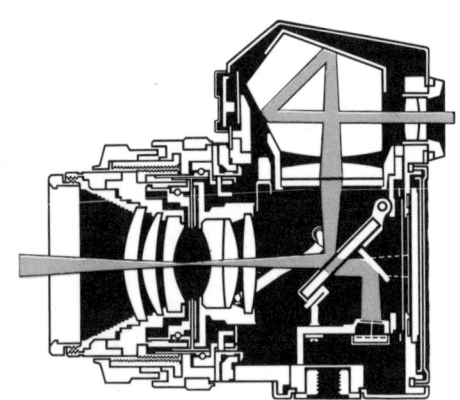

Parallax problems do not exist with the single-lens reflex camera, for the lens itself serves as the viewfinder.

Photographing plants

With supplementary lenses one can take plants in close-up – at less than one metre's distance – with almost any camera. Supplementary lenses are cheap and do not require any additional exposure time. They give the best picture quality at distances over 30 cm with *f* 8 or 11. In order to focus without bother and to keep control of the composition of the picture, we work with a tripod and cable release. In close-up photography the viewfinder parallax must be borne in mind, for the viewfinder, being higher than the lens, shows a different section of the subject. Single-lens reflex cameras do not suffer from this problem. In close-up photographs there is a very considerable displacement; at greater distances the displacement of the picture is much less and does not cause problems. The background is particularly important. Flowers seem

less brightly coloured when photographed against the sky than when shown against a dark background (see page 33).
We can also allow the background to go out of focus, if we calculate the depth of field properly, and if we shade the background with a hand, our flowers will also stand out brilliantly. The simplest solution is to make the flowers dominate the picture and to fill the whole picture format with them.

Mountain photography

The best mountain pictures are taken in the morning and evening. Then interesting shadow formations give relief and depth to the picture. Before we begin our own photography, let's first have a quiet look at the picture postcards of a particular area. We will know then which mountain views are favourite postcard subjects. Panoramic shots suit the landscape format; dizzy depths and majestic heights the upright.

For the greatest impact we must have something to show the scale. The most convincing evidence in a landscape picture is a human being. For picture depth have trees, stones and flowers in the foreground. Distant mountains look far too small in photographs. Lakes with mountains in the background result in exciting and beautiful photographs which are very popular on calendars.

When we show reflections of mountains, clouds and people in a lake, then it must be clear that they are reflections. The origin of the reflection must also be included.

Climbing pictures are always effective taken straight down – for an impression of depth – or straight up, into the sky. Don't forget that the higher you go, the more essential does a UV filter become. Above 2500 m it is a must.

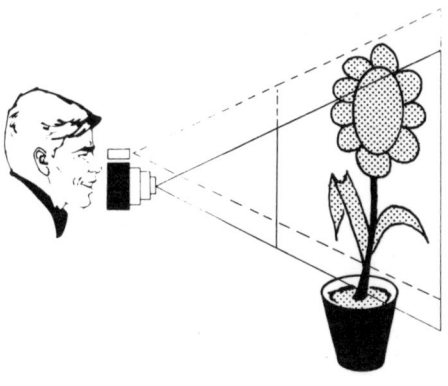

Parallax
The viewfinder is in a slightly different position from the angle of view of the lens. So the eye sees the subject from a somewhat different angle from the lens. The solution is to tilt the camera upwards, in the direction of the viewfinder, so that no important part of the picture is lost.

In snow and ice

Snow has too little contrast, even in sunshine, for black-and-white films. We can strengthen the contrast with a yellow filter and exaggerate it with an orange one.

Side lighting is good and against-the-light is even better. We should concentrate on close-ups and study how the lines run in the picture. When snow accounts for more than 70 per cent of the picture, we must double the exposure given by the exposure meter. With colour photography we can suppress UV light in high regions with a filter, and so avoid the danger of a blue cast.

Tripod

If you have a tripod, you can take time over your photography. You can achieve perfect focus and, with long exposures and stationary subjects, you can take pictures which would be impossible with a hand-held camera. Ideally the tripod should not be too light, the lens should be powerful and the film fast.
For tripod photography we need a cable release. It must be long enough to prevent vibrations from our hand reaching the camera. A cable release of less than 200 mm is useless.

Photographs by candlelight:
The subject should not be moving and you should use a long exposure, a tripod and a cable release.

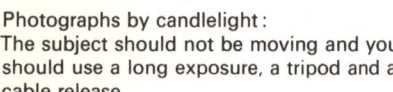

Portrait photography

Before we dare tackle a portrait, we must think how the person portrayed can be shown in a fresh, lively and realistic way. Everyone has his best side which we must discover. We must also remember that most people know themselves only as mirror images. The photograph which shows them the right way round is often a disappointment because it is unfamiliar. The most important thing for lively portraits is to divert and occupy the person we want to photograph. For most people are camera-shy and they adopt the all too familiar rigid "camera face". It was to give their pictures a relaxed air that the old photographers made their subjects say "cheese", just as they released the shutter. Before we make the exposure, we should check that no part of the body is too close to the camera. We want to avoid hands or knees which are out of proportion. To avoid distorted perspectives, we should not approach nearer than 1.50 m. Remember too that clothing and background should not be distracting, and, if possible, the sitter should never wear sun glasses. Watch out for irritating reflections when photographing spectacle wearers. Raising the head emphasizes the mouth and lowering it emphasizes the eyes. The best portraits are snapshots. The most effective lighting is midway between side and front lighting. True against-the-light gives silhouettes. If we want to use flash, then we should hold the flash to the side of the camera at an angle of 30 to 45°, for, if we were to use the flash on the camera, the portrait would be flat and lacking in modelling.

When we photograph people, we should position ourselves on the same level as our subjects. Children should not be "looked down to" and adults do not have to be "looked up to". It may be, of course, that one wants to use these techniques to make things look smaller or larger. And when we have got our victim in our clutches, let's take a whole series of photographs. One picture at least is bound to be satisfactory and we can learn from the rest.

Still-life and table-top photography

Under the heading of still life in painting and photography comes the presentation of things such as flowers and fruit, which are lifeless or stationary. We don't want to compose classical still lifes but to train our eye to take photographs of objects arranged to form attractive scenes. In this we can show our skill in composition. A feeling for colour and good lighting technique are particularly important. To avoid unplanned areas of unsharpness, we must study the depth-of-field tables for our camera with great care. We should decide on the smallest aperture possible so that the maximum area of the picture is sharp. In doubtful cases use a tape measure. Before making the exposure, check that there are no reflections from shining surfaces, and that there are no distorted perspectives. To prevent unwanted light from spoiling the brilliance of our photograph, we should use a lens hood on the camera. We must remember too that for colour transparencies we need an artificial light film.

The star effect is obtained in against-the-light photography by stopping the lens right down.

Rest the camera on something or use a tripod and cable release. A long exposure is needed. It would be even more effective if taken at twilight, as the outlines of the houses and of the girders of the bridge could be picked out.

Winning friends through photography.

Before we say goodbye

If you want to be a serious photographer — and perhaps one day a professional photo-journalist or fashion photographer — you will find all you need to know about the theory and practice of photography in either the books of Andreas Feininger (published by Thames & Hudson) or in *The Penguin Handbook of Photography* by Eric de Maré.
There are also a number of excellent photographic magazines such as *Popular Photography* and *Modern Photography* (both imported from the United States).

Beach photography

If we should want to make a particularly boring picture, we would divide it into two equal sections. For interesting pictures I would advise two-thirds beach and one third sky, that is, if something is happening on the beach. If the cloud formations are especially interesting, then reverse this. Above all, something should be happening in the foreground. Fishing boats, sun umbrellas, beach chairs — there are plenty of subjects, and don't forget the people on the beach with their sun-tanned bodies. They are particularly photogenic when they are shining with water or sun oil; otherwise they look a bit flat. If we try to take colour photographs at midday, we run the risk of a blue cast. We can get round this by using a UV or skylight filter.
The morning produces good pictures but midday is an enemy to photography.

Architecture

When we want to photograph great buildings and churches, we must remember that flat lighting does not produce any modelling. We advise that the light should come from either side of the camera. We should stand back as far as possible so that there are as few distortions of perspective caused by converging lines as possible. We can, of course, exaggerate this convergence of vertical lines if we want. This produces striking pictorial effects. In taking pictures from the top of church towers and high buildings, we should tilt the camera forwards. Windows, doorways and arches in the foreground give the picture a frame through which distant fountains, statues and so on can be seen. Flights of steps offer a wide range of possibilities for interesting compositions. We should remember that details are often more striking and convincing than the whole. Don't point your exposure meter at the sky or your building will be under-exposed.

Sports

Capture the right instant. Often our reactions are not quick enough for this. We must trust to luck and shoot off a number of exposures, one of which will perhaps have caught the right situation, or else press the release before the decisive moment arrives.
There are types of sport in which the action stands still for a fraction of a second — for instance, in jumping. We wait for the decisive moment with our finger on the release.

Slower shutter speeds can be used if the camera is "panned". How does this work? During the exposure we swing the camera round in the same direction as the movement, so that the racehorse apparently stands still. The background is out of focus and gives the impression of tremendous action.

In sports photography it is not the actual speed which is important but the angle of the movement to the camera. Something which is moving towards the camera looks slow. Something moving at an oblique angle seems faster. The greatest impression of speed, however, is given when the movement is across the camera's field of vision.

Fireworks and lightning

Photographs of fireworks are impressive, capturing, as they do, the brief flare of the splendid clusters of light. To take pictures like this you don't need to be a professional photographer.

We must give a very long exposure and so also need a tripod and a cable release. We should choose an aperture between f 2.8 and 4 and a shutter speed of 2–6 seconds; then we will catch sufficient stars, without the risk of several stars blurring together or of light flare. It is very effective when silhouettes, lit from behind, of roofs, big wheels, or towers appear in the picture.

We can also, for instance, with 50 ASA films use f 8 and the B shutter setting and gather several flashes of lightning together in one picture by leaving the shutter open and shielding the lens between flashes with a hand or lens cap until we feel we have recorded enough.

Photographing television

Switch on as few lights as possible. Then adjust the television set not to bright but to high contrast and switch off any lights which cause disturbing reflections. Open the diaphragm up to f 2.8–4 and expose with a medium-speed film at a distance of 1 m and an exposure of 1/30 second.

We will not obtain especially good focus and brilliance in photographing television pictures, for the television picture is built up electronically of lines. We should therefore not give a shorter exposure than 1/30 second, for the electronic beam scans 50 half-pictures a second. Therefore, a speed faster than 1/50 would produce only a partial image.

Good luck!

The lens has a diaphragm and a shutter. We control the amount of light passing through the lens with the diaphragm.

We determine the length of the exposure with the shutter. The higher the shutter speed number, the shorter the exposure time — the lower the number, the longer the time.

Each camera is a light-tight box with a lens that passes light and a film which is sensitive to light.

The light has an exact strength. We can estimate it with the help of exposure tables or, better still, measure it with an exposure meter.

The exposure meter provides us with combinations of apertures and speeds which give good exposures related to the speed of the film.

The film has an exact speed or light-sensitivity which is expressed in ASA. As the ASA number is doubled, so is the film speed.

The film renders colours as tones of grey in black-and-white photographs. If we want colour pictures we use colour negative or colour reversal films.